Wave after wave rolls onto the rocky coast at Crescent Beach   TERRY DONNELLY

" *This far-famed Oregon, and indeed, all of this portion of the Pacific Coast differs so much from any other part of the United States that the best geographic description that can be given of it will impart but a feeble idea of the reality, to one that has never beheld it . . . . A climate that imparts vigor and robust health . . . . Delightful groves of fir, spruce and white cedar that are unsurpassed in the world, mountain streams without number . . . a fertility of soil that commends itself to every settler as being all that could be desired . . . . You have before you the Territory of Oregon, combining in a degree seldom met with the Beautiful with the Practical. This is the Territory of which you ask me to give you a detailed description! The task looms up like the Cascade Range . . . .* "*

A. N. Armstrong,
in a letter to a friend
while writing *The History of Oregon*, 1856

Mount Hood rises above a wildflower-spangled alpine meadow LARRY GEDDIS

The sparse beauty of the desert at Abert Rim in Lake County   LARRY GEDDIS

The Crooked River flows through a canyon of basalt north of Redmond   BARRY PERIL

The rugged east face of Steens Mountain looms over an ephemeral desert lake in Harney County   WAYNE ALDRIDGE

66 *Stand at the top of Steens Mountain, look far away into five states, look nearly straight down to the beautiful Alvord Ranch, then look carefully around at the Alpine wild flowers. Try to take the time to sit down and watch how sunshine and shadow first color, then wipe out and recolor the scene. This is a good place to think about America for a few hours. Maybe this is what our mountain has to offer: enduring beauty, quiet, and blessed solitude. Those things aren't listed among the seven thousand items in a supermarket. Here the poorest may purchase as much as the richest.* 99

E. R. Jackman,
Steens Mountain in Oregon's High Desert Country

The fantastic hues of the Painted Hills at John Day Fossil Beds National Monument
glow beneath a brooding sky   STEVE TERRILL

> *It's the great, big, broad land 'way up yonder,*
> *It's the forests where silence has lease;*
> *It's the beauty that thrills me with wonder,*
> *It's the stillness that fills me with peace.*

Robert Service,
The Spell of the Yukon

Mule deer buck ALAN D. ST. JOHN

Tanner Creek flows through a lush rain forest in the Columbia River Gorge   GERRY ELLIS

66 Green is the color of Western Oregon; water is the vital fluid in the paint. 99

Marnie McPhee,
Western Oregon: Portrait of the Land and its People

A mushroom sprouts from the desert floor along Tanner Creek
GERRY ELLIS

The waters of Lower Proxy Falls cascade over mossy rocks west of Mckenzie Pass in Willamette National Forest JEFF GNASS

Mount Jefferson dominates the skyline in the Mount Jefferson Wilderness Area   STEVE TERRILL

Rhododendrons and shore pines fight a fruitless battle against advancing sand at the Oregon Dunes National Recreation Area   WILLARD CLAY

Pacific tree frog   TOM & PAT LEESON

The Sokol–Blosser Vineyard in Yamhill County WAYNE ALDRIDGE

> *It's almost as if the valley had been built just to grow food. Its broad bottom, gently sloping to the north at an average of two feet per mile, slows down the rivers and streams that empty into the basin; even at flood, they drop their alluvium, building thick soil.*

Marnie McPhee,
Western Oregon: Portrait of the Land and Its People

Pinot Noir grapes ripen on the vine in Dundee
WAYNE ALDRIDGE

Corn grows tall and fast under the hot August sun   CHARLIE BORELAND/BORELAND STOCK PHOTO

Autumn bounty in the Willamette Valley CHARLIE BORELAND/BORELAND STOCK PHOTO

Helping with the harvest
CHARLIE BORELAND/BORELAND STOCK PHOTO

Autumn chores on the farm
KERRY WETZEL/BORELAND STOCK PHOTO

Rows of beans parade across a Willamette Valley landscape   STEVE TERRILL

Red clover graces a field in Yamhill County   LARRY GEDDIS

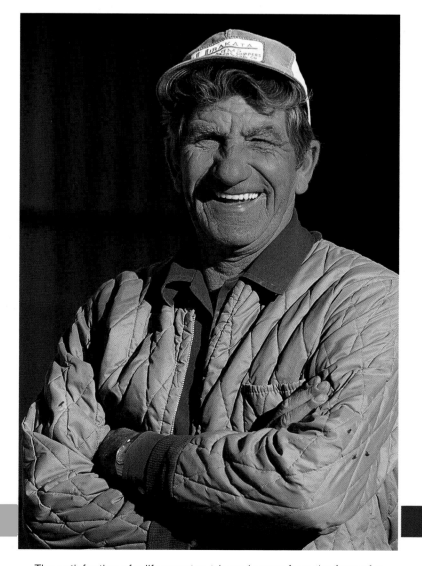

If you ask a farmer anywhere in the world to describe the perfect conditions for farming, their requirements would most likely fit the Willamette Valley.

Archie Satterfield,
Country Roads of Oregon

The satisfaction of a life spent outdoors beams from the face of a
Willamette Valley farmer   BRYAN PETERSON/BORELAND STOCK PHOTO

A country lane near Prairie City heads toward the Strawberry Mountains STEVE TERRILL

A farm with a view in the Wallowa Valley   DAVID JENSEN

Raising Old Glory at the Saint Paul Mission Historical Society
GREG VAUGHN

Oregon is a rural retreat with an inbred aversion to moneyed flamboyance and prep school arrogance. But some impressions fail to capture one important aspect of Oregon. Oregon is a state of home builders, not empire builders.

Ken Metzler,
The Best of Oregon

A fisherman makes the last cast of the day in the gathering darkness at Mann Lake   DENNIS FRATES

66 *The steelhead has become a fish of
legend in tales told around the campfires
that flicker on countless riverbanks in the
raining dawn, or in tall stories swapped over
steaming cups of coffee in the greasy-spoon
diners of little towns clustered along the
rivers. There are other great fishing
traditions, but none quite the same as this.* 99

Steve Raymond,
Steelhead Country

23

A fly box well stocked with steelhead flies
BRIAN O'KEEFE

A steelhead fisherman patiently casts for his elusive quarry on the North Umpqua River   BRIAN O'KEEFE

66 Downstream the water is pure chaos, a riot of silver, the crushing of water and air. Upstream, a black agate pool, a water glide of anthracite, the falling of the verge . . . . Caught between depression and disaster, this river valley holds us in her soft emerald hands. In this double vision afternoon, the summer steelhead sit and wait, the forest lies down with the river and the sky falls in on me. How a river comes to be a lover and loved. It was so much more than a one-fish afternoon. 99

Peter Coyne,
from "OREGON: North Fork of Umpqua River"
in *Trout* magazine

Making a catch on Trillium Lake in Mount Hood National Forest STEVE WANKE/BORELAND STOCK PHOTO

In search of trout on the spring-fed Metolius River
BRIAN O'KEEFE

Persistence has paid off for this Deschutes River
steelhead fisherman BRIAN O'KEEFE

The Pacific Ocean meets Oregon at Shore Acres State Park LARRY GEDDIS

66 In terms of ruggedness, few coastlines match Oregon's battered brow. The waves push unimpeded across 6,000 miles of ocean in a headlong assault, their nibbling crests equal in height to a two-story building, striking basaltic rock with the force of a thousand logging trucks. The land gives, falls back, surrenders—but slowly—to ceaseless abrasion and thunderous uppercuts that send water and air whistling through rock cracks like an explosive fuel mixture in a compressing cylinder. 99

Peter Jensen,
The Coast of Oregon

Well-weathered driftwood litters the beach at
Cape Blanco State Park TERRY DONNELLY

Fog brushes the tops of the trees as it lifts above the coast near Port Orford   STEVE TERRILL

Wild dock plants frame a view of the Pacific Ocean at Samuel H. Boardman State Park   STEVE TERRILL

California sea lions haul out onto a rock to sun themselves   TOM & PAT LEESON

Coquille Lighthouse stands sentry at the mouth of the Coquille River just north of Bandon WILLARD CLAY

A profusion of goose barnacles cling to a seashore rock
DONNA IKENBERRY AITKENHEAD

" Here are three hundred miles of pictures of rock and water in black and white, or gray and white, with more or less of green and yellow, purple and blue. The rocks, glistening in sunshine and foam, are never wholly dry— many of them marvels of wave- sculpture and most imposing in bulk and bearing, standing boldly forward, monuments of a thousand storms, types of permanence, holding the homes and places of refuge of multitudes of seafaring animals in their keeping, yet ever wasting away. "

John Muir,
Steep Trails

An expanse of sand dune near Myers Creek at Pistol River State Park   STEVE TERRILL

Ocean-scoured sandstone, Cape Arago State Park   CHARLIE BORELAND/BORELAND STOCK PHOTO

Work goes on late into the night at a Portland shipyard   CHARLIE BORELAND/BORELAND STOCK PHOTO

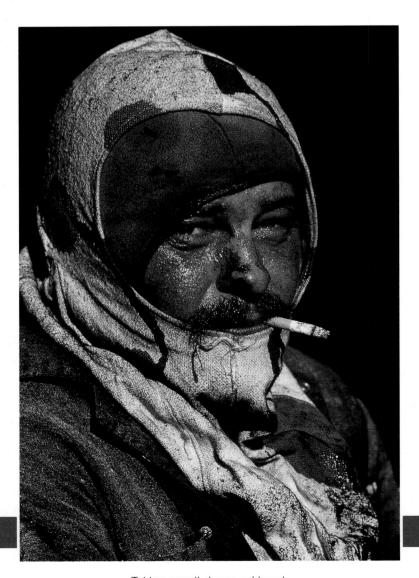

Taking a well-deserved break
CHARLIE BORELAND/BORELAND STOCK PHOTO

Columbia River dams produce the Pacific Northwest's electricity BRYAN PETERSON/BORELAND STOCK PHOTO

A foundry worker labors between fire and flame BRYAN PETERSON/BORELAND STOCK PHOTO

Fiber optics: high-tech industries have arrived in Oregon GARY TARLETON/BORELAND STOCK PHOTO

A worker tugs at Gulliver-sized chains at a Portland shipyard   BRYAN PETERSON/BORELAND STOCK PHOTO

Fishing nets lie in a pile along the docks at Newport's Yaquina Bay   TERRY DONNELLY

Fishing boats set out to sea with flocks of hungry gulls in tow
BRYAN PETERSON/BORELAND STOCK PHOTO

Docked fishing boats at Coos Bay in late afternoon light   TERRY DONNELLY

A gull stations himself on a pier piling   GREG VAUGHN

" Down the dock ramps, below the fish-house and the church, the fishing boats lay moored and felt the sound from a mile out. They rocked and rubbed the docks with their rubber tire bumpers, waltzing their troller poles back and forth to the undeniable tune of the sea. "

Ken Kesey,
from "The First Sunday in September"
in *The World Begins Here:
An Anthology of Oregon Short Fiction*

An Oregon coast sunset   BRYAN PETERSON/BORELAND STOCK PHOTO

A basalt arch on Saint Peter's dome above the Columbia River Gorge National Scenic Area   STEVE TERRILL

Outcroppings of pumice have been eroded into weirdly shaped pinnacles at Crater Lake National Park   WAYNE ALDRIDGE

Autumn in the Mount Jefferson Wilderness Area STEVE TERRILL

A wood duck drake in his resplendent glory J. C. MILLER

It is fall in Oregon. On the coast, the shortened days bring signs of 'wintering in' to the human and animal residents who will be there when January storms unleash nature's harshness. In the Columbia River Gorge, a gentle mist settles on the ridgetops and breathes moisture into the valley below. Snow—a blanketing peace to earth—seeks the upper reaches of the Wallowas, driving the deer and elk to lower havens. In central Oregon, nights are cold and clear and the nocturnal yowl of a coyote touches off endless wanderings of the mind. On Willamette Pass, vine maple and alder join other flora to emblazen the hillsides with rich hues of yellow, gold, red, orange and brown. In Lakeview, a falling cottonwood leaf twirls through patches of sunlight and shadow, catches an updraft for a wild moment, then quietly caresses earth.

Thomas K. Worcester,
A Portrait of Oregon

Vine maples engulf Douglas-firs in fiery autumn colors JEFF GNASS

The western tanager is a common bird of the Oregon forest DONALD M. JONES

A touch of fall color punctuates an old-growth forest along the Oak Fork of the Clackamas River   GEORGE WUERTHNER

A wintery moon rises over Mount Hood JEFF GNASS

" *There stood Mount Hood in all the glory of the alpenglow, looming immensely high, beaming with intelligence, and so impressive that one was overawed as if suddenly brought before some superior being newly arrived from the sky.* "

John Muir,
Steep Trails

The historic Timberline Lodge nestles at the base of Mount Hood   LARRY GEDDIS

A downhill skier catches some air
MIKE BELOZER/BORELAND STOCK PHOTO

A mountaineer descends Mount Hood on a perfect winter day   JON GNASS

Winter fun   BRYAN PETERSON/BORELAND STOCK PHOTO

The bright lights of Portland twinkle beneath Mount Hood   JEFF GNASS

Lovely in the daytime, the city is magic at night! Lights dance in the velvety, black Willamette River and laughter floats on the breeze. Rickshaw rides are offered by brawny legged young men who run so swiftly that passengers have the sense of flying. Music drifts from nightclubs which overflow with enthusiasts who are just happy to dance outside on the sidewalk.

Leslie Rule,
Beautiful America's Portland

Portland's Oregon History Center is a repository of Oregon's rich heritage RICK SCHAFER

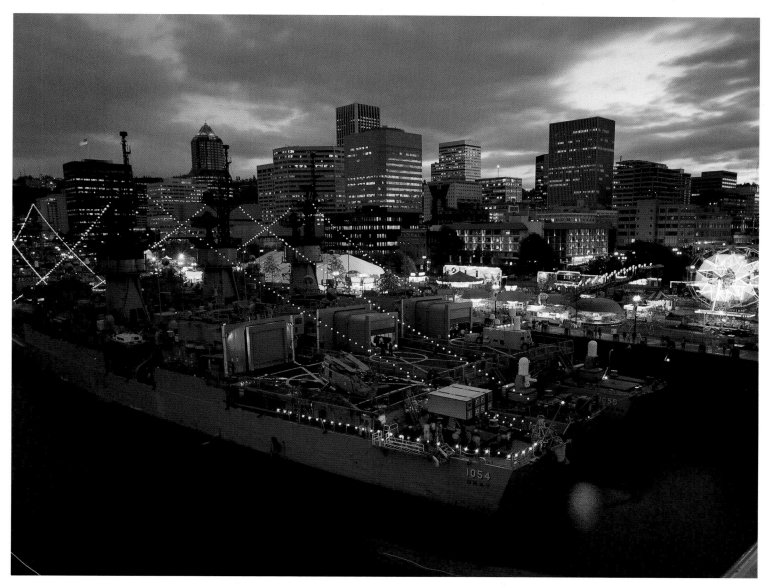

Navy ships dock at Portland's bustling Willamette River waterfront   RICK SCHAFER

Umbrellas bloom like poppies on the rainy winter
streets of Portland   GREG VAUGHN

" *Without sounding too corny or sentimental about it–and well aware of pressing social and environmental problems–my hunch is that if Plato were around today, writing* The City *instead of* The Republic, *he'd come up with a plan along the lines of Portland, an urban environment where a person can still move with relative ease through the private and public realms of life.* "

Doug Marx,
Willamette Week

53

The Festival of Flowers in Portland, the "City of Roses" LARRY GEDDIS

> *"Portland is a lovely, youthful woman—with, of course—roses in her cheeks, roses in her arms, and roses tucked in her luxuriant hair. Portland is gracious, friendly, and polite to strangers—but watch her closely. She's winking at you."*
>
> Leslie Rule,
> *Beautiful America's Portland*

A parade in Portland's Chinatown STEVE TERRILL

Fireworks sizzle over the Willamette River during Portland's annual Fourth of July celebration   STEVE TERRILL

Fort Clatsop National Memorial, near Astoria, reconstructs the site where Lewis and Clark spent the winter of 1805–1806   LARRY GEDDIS

" Astoria itself looks down river upon an infinity of water that is still for a long time the Columbia before it becomes the Pacific Ocean. "

Roderick Haig-Brown,
from "Spring the Salmon Reaches the Ocean"
in *Varieties of Hope: An Anthology of Oregon Prose*

The 125-foot-high Astoria Column was erected in 1926 to honor the Lewis and Clark expedition   JEFF GNASS

The Astoria bridge spans the Columbia River between Oregon and Washington   WAYNE MICHAEL LOTTINVILLE/N.E. STOCK PHOTO

The Columbia, one of America's great rivers, rolls to sea TERRY DONNELLY

" *It's a land of anomalies and paradoxes, one which must have puzzled Lewis and Clark when, in 1805, they became the first white men to traverse the Columbia River Gorge. They must have wondered about this river that, rather than flowing down and around the mountains, simply tunneled through them.* "

Andy Dappen,
from "Backroads Revisited"
in *Pacific Northwest* magazine

The Columbia River Gorge has been designated a National Scenic Area   JEFF GNASS

Visitors get a bird's-eye view of Multnomah Falls in the Columbia River Gorge   WAYNE ALDRIDGE

The historic Columbia River Scenic Highway winds through a lush forest landscape LARRY GEDDIS

A curious raccoon GERRY ELLIS

Mount Jefferson and bear grass at Scout Lake   TERRY DONNELLY

A black-tailed deer fawn hides among forest vegetation
TOM & PAT LEESON

The Rabbit Ears, Rogue River National Forest STEVE TERRILL

A grand view from North Point in the Bridge Creek Wilderness Area   STEVE TERRILL

❝ Oregon is still one of the privileged places with vast, empty, silent spaces, beautiful and remote. ❞

Paul M. Lewis,
Beauty of Oregon

Sunset casts a golden glow on Shiprock STEVE TERRILL

Ocean-carved cliffs along the coast at Otter Crest WAYNE ALDRIDGE

The Oregon Coast displays a majesty that captures your spirit. There is such power in the coast's beauty, the crashing rhythm of its waves, the immensity of towering Douglas fir or Sitka spruce, and craggy upthrust shores—power in the seeming perpetuity of coastal splendor. With that everlasting quality comes a peaceful essence, too, that feeling bestowed when you have the chance to sit and watch waves lapping against a rising sun or fog slinking through the trees as it is being chased by a breeze.

Linda Sterling-Wanner,
Beautiful America's Oregon Coast

Sea stacks mirrored in the wet sand at Devils Elbow State Park   TERRY DONNELLY

Tufted puffins are clownlike denizens of
coastal headlands   TOM & PAT LEESON

Sea stars, anemones, and mussels vie for space in a tidepool GREG VAUGHN

A remnant of the Oregon Trail descends to Virgin Flat, southwest of Flagstaff Hill   GARY LADD

The open Barlow Road tollgate and a forest beckon wanderers down the old Oregon Trail   GREG VAUGHN

Wagons still roll across the rangelands of eastern Oregon   DAVID JENSEN

66 First just a trickle, then the trickle became a flow as hundreds of men, women and children moved across the plains to the promised land at the end of the longest wagon road in history . . . . It was on to Oregon, and a spirit seldom equalled in the transition of man. 99

Thomas K. Worcester,
A Portrait of Oregon

Moving cattle through the open range near Madras   STEVE TERRILL

Crow's feet and squint marks were chiseled into the hammered-copper face of the cowboy and steady eyes met the gaze of a stranger openly. His faded jeans, checkered shirt, pointed boots and curl-brimmed straw hat were his uniform, and he stood at the jackpine corral, one foot on a lower rail, as he answered the question with a good-natured patience. 'Travel? Where would I go? This is Oregon—I'm already there.'

Thomas K. Worcester,
A Portrait of Oregon

A rancher surveys his herd near Antelope   STEVE TERRILL

Cowboys share a campfire and the silence of the range at the end of a hard day   STEVE WANKE/BORELAND STOCK PHOTO

The Owyhee River carves out a spectacular gorge in the remote reaches of southeast Oregon   DAVID JENSEN

The Powder River flows through lonely country in Baker County   DENNIS FRATES

A pronghorn antelope, fleet-footed runner
of the high plains   DONALD M. JONES

66 *Valleys are as flat as a table top for seventy-five miles. The land is bleak and gray. Yet a shimmer of blue against the skyline says that there is water to be had. A streak of green along a distant hillside tells of springs and creeks. Patches of light green across the plateaus show where rich native hay grows. And one has only to watch the plateau through glasses or walk through its sagebrush to learn that it virtually teems with life. This is land to embrace. It is land to command as far as the eye can see.* 99

William O. Douglas,
Varieties of Hope: An Anthology of Oregon Prose

The Hood River Valley is renowned for its apple orchards   FRED PFLUGHOFT

66 Imagine traveling up the Hood River Valley during apple blossom time, when the valley is resplendent with blooming orchards. Or in summer and early fall when the fruit ripens and delicious scents waft into the river canyon. 99

Andy Dappen,
from "Tickets to Paradise"
in *Pacific Northwest* magazine

A Hood River Valley harvest   TOM & PAT LEESON

Flowering pear trees in the fertile Hood River Valley STEVE TERRILL

A spring snowfall dusts skunk cabbage in a Coast Range forest   TOM & PAT LEESON

Deer fern fiddleheads slowly unfurl as spring comes upon the land   GERRY ELLIS

Monkey flowers, lupines, and Indian paintbrush dress up a mountain stream   STEVE TERRILL

Dad and kids explore Sparks Lake beneath the shadow of the South Sister peak GREG VAUGHN

" To be in Oregon is to be outdoors. "

Thomas K. Worcester,
A Portrait of Oregon

A youngster proudly shows off his catch of the day
BRIAN O'KEEFE

Sailboarders prepare to ride the wind CHARLIE BORELAND/BORELAND STOCK PHOTO

Oregonians work hard and play hard   BRIAN DRAKE

The Columbia River Gorge's constant, brisk winds make it a mecca for sailboarding   BRIAN BELOZER/BORELAND STOCK PHOTO

A long hike is rewarded with a spectacular view of the North and Middle Sisters
in the Three Sisters Wilderness Area   JON GNASS

You can hike to the clouds in Oregon CHARLIE BORELAND/BORELAND STOCK PHOTO

A contestant rolls across the finish line in the
Hood to Coast Relay GREG VAUGHN

*Oregonians have always been proud of
their state, to the point, let us be frank, of
considering themselves special.*

Win McCormack,
*Profiles of Oregon: An Anthology
of Articles from* Oregon *magazine*

Loggers ply their trade deep in the forest   CHARLIE BORELAND/BORELAND STOCK PHOTO

The timber worker has made Oregon much of what it is today CHARLIE BORELAND/BORELAND STOCK PHOTO

Raw logs are shipped abroad from the busy port at Coos Bay
GALEN ROWELL

66 The logger comes in all sizes, from small to very large, and in all dispositions, from surly to downright amiable. His color, which may be white, brown, black or red is unimportant since it is usually smeared with oil, dirt and sweat . . . . He may speak with a New England twang, a Southern drawl, the sing-song of Norway, a Scottish burr, or some completely unintelligible growl, but each and every man has one common unifying trait: The logger is the proudest man alive. 99

Earl Roberge,
Timber Country

In Clackamas County, the Sandy River is drenched in fog STEVE TERRILL

A small mountain lake graces a forest opening in Mount Hood National Forest STEVE TERRILL

A black bear cub scrambles up a tree to safety TOM & PAT LEESON

“ *Fog ravels down from the pine needles. Above, up through the branches, the sky is blue and still and very clear, but fog is on the land.* ”

Ken Kesey,
Sometimes a Great Notion

Big Lake and Mount Washington in the stillness of the Cascade Mountains   STEVE TERRILL

Mule deer are often spotted on the shores of Wallowa Lake in Oregon's far northeast corner   LARRY GEDDIS

A blackbird's nest is tucked away in the marsh reeds
ALAN D. ST. JOHN

Harbinger of spring, a male red-winged blackbird
perches on a cattail   DONALD M. JONES

Opal Creek, in Willamette National Forest, is the site of one of Oregon's last, best ancient forests   STEVE TERRILL

A rough-skinned newt in breeding coloration crawls
across the forest floor   JIM YUSKAVITCH

North Falls in Silver Creek State Park   WILLARD CLAY

A rare Pacific fisher peers out from
the dark forest   ART WOLFE

A chickaree dines on a fir cone   TOM & PAT LEESON

Wizard Island rises out of the crystalline waters of Crater Lake National Park   LARRY GEDDIS

" Upon seeing the lake, it's impossible not to wonder how in the world something so beautiful ever came to be. "

Donna Ikenberry Aitkenhead,
from "Cycling Crater Lake National Park"
in *Bike Report* magazine

Gray jay   DONNA IKENBERRY AITKENHEAD

Winter's stark majesty cloaks Mount Washington   LARRY GEDDIS

Sunrise bathes the South Sister in a warm alpenglow in the Three Sisters Wilderness Area   FRED PFLUGHOFT

Tundra swans launch themselves into flight from Malheur National Wildlife Refuge   TOM & PAT LEESON

Winter along Eagle Creek in the Salmon–Huckleberry Wilderness in Mount Hood National Forest   WAYNE ALDRIDGE

Mount Hood National Forest's Sandy River in frigid splendor   STEVE TERRILL

Skiers flock to Oregon's mountains each winter   R. M. COLLINS III

A pair of snowboarders take in a little winter sunshine   CHARLIE BORELAND/BORELAND STOCK PHOTO

Backcountry campers spend Christmas Eve near Mount Hood   CHARLIE BORELAND/BORELAND STOCK PHOTO

A climber is rewarded with a grand vista of the Eagle Cap
Wilderness Area   SUE PFLUGHOFT

Oregon's ancient forests are places of magic STEVE MOHLENKAMP

Dawn greets the Oregon Coast at Cape Perpetua   STEVE MOHLENKAMP

> *" The Wallowa area is such a beautiful end-of-the-road kind of place that nearly everyone who visits it comes to think of it as their own personal secret. "*

Archie Satterfield,
Country Roads of Oregon

A bald eagle surveys his domain TOM & PAT LEESON

Sunshine Lake reflects the rugged granite peaks in the Eagle Cap Wilderness Area   LARRY GEDDIS

Oneonta Gorge is a fairyland of water, ferns, and mosses   JEFF GNASS

Toketee Falls plummets into the North Umpqua River in Douglas County   WAYNE ALDRIDGE

The "Monkey Face" is a distinctive rock formation at Smith Rock State Park   R. M. COLLINS III

A rock climber scales a cliff at Smith Rock State Park
CHARLIE BORELAND/BORELAND STOCK PHOTO

The Crooked River winds its way through the gorge at Smith Rock State Park   LARRY GEDDIS

Groves of immense redwoods grow in the forests of Oregon's southern coast   GERRY ELLIS

A Roosevelt's elk bull wanders through a meadow   TOM & PAT LEESON

The varied hues of Indian paintbrush   DAVID JENSEN

" California is world-famous for its immense stands of coastal redwoods, giants that reach for the sky, tallest living trees on earth. But Oregon has some giants of its own, and they are just as beautiful and just as awesome. "

Donna Ikenberry Aitkenhead, from
"Bicycling Oregon's Redwoods"
in *Oregon Coast* magazine

Stormclouds gather over the John Day River   DENNIS FRATES

Fort Rock, formed by ancient volcanic activity, stands in a sea of sagebrush in Lake County   STEVE TERRILL

Rabbitbrush in bloom adds color to the desert landscape around Lake Owyhee in Malheur County   GREG VAUGHN

"The soft and wooly, gently rolling
Sagebrush desert. . . . . .
A prayer-carpet spread by God
For the stars to walk on."

John W. Evans,
"Night on the Desert" in *Oregon East*

The vibrant hues of Portland's Japanese Gardens delight the eye   WILLARD CLAY

Wisteria hangs wistfully above a park bench in Portland   LARRY GEDDIS

The state Capitol in Salem LARRY GEDDIS

Splashes of colorful flowers vibrate on a misty western Oregon morning at Shore Acres State Park   STEVE TERRILL

A fragrant bouquet, reflected in raindrops   STEVE TERRILL

A praying mantis, friend of gardeners   J. C. MILLER

they made it possible

Oregon on My mind would have been impossible to produce without the keen eyes and technical skills of more than thirty professional photographers. These men and women submitted their finest images, and the result shows in this stunning collection of photos. What does not show is the work it took to get these images—the early mornings to capture the sunrise, the long climbs through rugged terrain, the endless hours of waiting for the perfect light, the hundreds of shots that didn't turn out quite right, and the high level of technical skills that were aquired through years of experience and study. To all the photographers who contributed to *Oregon on My Mind*, we say thanks. We appreciate their art and their hard work.

Michael S. Sample and Bill Schneider
Publishers

Photographers in *Oregon on My Mind*

Donna Ikenberry Aitkenhead
Wayne Aldridge
Mike Belozer
Charlie Boreland
Willard Clay
R. M. Collins III
Terry Donnelly
Brian Drake
Gerry Ellis
Dennis Frates
Larry Geddis
Jeff Gnass
Jon Gnass
David Jensen
Donald M. Jones
Gary Ladd
Russell Lamb
Tom & Pat Leeson
Wayne Michael Lottinville
J. C. Miller
Steve Mohlenkamp

Brian O'Keefe
Barry Peril
Bryan Peterson
Fred Pflughoft
Sue Pflughoft
Galen Rowell
Rick Schafer
Ty Smedes
Alan D. St. John
Gary Tarleton
Steve Terrill
Greg Vaughn
Steve Wanke
Kerry Wetzel
George Wuerthner
Art Wolfe
Jim Yuskavitch

Boreland Stock Photo
N.E. Stock Photo

Copyright © 1995 by Falcon®Publishing, Inc. Helena, Montana

All rights reserved, including the right to reproduce any part of this book in any form, except brief quotations for reviews, without the written permission of the publisher.

Design, typesetting, and other prepress work by Falcon Publishing, Helena, Montana. Printed in Korea.

Library of Congress Number: 94-71772

ISBN 1-56044-307-3

For extra copies of this book please check with your local bookstore, or write to Falcon, P.O. Box 1718, Helena, MT 59624 or call toll-free 1-800-582-2665.

Title page:
Sunrise from Lookout Point   DENNIS FRATES
End papers:
Ponderosa forest   FRED PFLUGHOLF

acknowledgments

The publisher gratefully acknowledges the following sources:

Pages 3, 10, 15 from *Western Oregon: Portrait of the Land and its People*, by Marnie McPhee. Copyright © 1987 by American Geographic Publishing, Helena, Montana.

Page 7 from *Steens Mountain in Oregon's High Desert Country*, by E. R. Jackman. Copyright © 1967 by The Caxton Printers, Ltd., Caldwell, Idaho.

Page 9 from *The Spell of the Yukon*, by Robert Service. Copyright © 1904 by Dodd, Mead & Company, New York.

Pages 19, 104 from *Country Roads of Oregon*, by Archie Satterfield. Copyright © 1993 by Country Roads Press, Castine, Maine.

Page 21 from *The Best of Oregon*, by Ken Metzler. Copyright © 1986 by Timber Press, Portland, Oregon.

Page 23 from *Steelhead Country*, by Steve Raymond. Copyright © 1991 by Lyons & Burford, Publishers, New York.

Page 24 from "Oregon: North Fork of Umpqua River," by Peter Coyne. Published in *Trout*, Spring 1989.

Page 26 from *The Coast of Oregon*, by Peter Jensen. Copyright © 1985 by Oxford University Press, Toronto.

Pages 29, 47 from *Steep Trails*, by John Muir. Copyright © 1918 by Houghton Mifflin Company, Boston.

Page 37 from "The First Sunday in September," by Ken Kesey, in *The World Begins Here: An Anthology of Oregon Short Fiction*. Copyright © 1993 by Oregon Council of Teachers of English; Oregon State University Press, Corvallis, Oregon.

Pages 43, 71, 73, 81 from *A Portrait of Oregon*, by Thomas K. Worcester, edited by Robert B. Pamplin, Jr. Copyright © 1973 by Oregon Museum of Science and Industry Press, Portland, Oregon.

Pages 51, 54 from *Beautiful America's Portland*, by Leslie Rule. Copyright © 1989 by Beautiful America Publishing Company, Portland, Oregon.

Page 53 from *Willamette Week*, November 2-8, 1989 by Doug Marx.

Page 56 from "Spring the Salmon Reaches the Ocean," by Roderick Haig-Brown, in *Varieties of Hope: An Anthology of Oregon Prose*, edited by Gordon B. Dodds. Copyright © 1993 by Oregon Council of Teachers of English; Oregon State University Press, Corvallis, Oregon.

Page 58 from "Backroads Revisited," by Andy Dappen. Published in *Pacific Northwest*, June 1989.

Page 64 from *Beauty of Oregon*, by Paul M. Lewis. Copyright © 1989 by LTA Publishing Company, Portland, Oregon.

Page 67 from *Beautiful America's Oregon Coast*, by Linda Sterling-Wanner. Copyright © 1991 by Beautiful America Publishing Company, Wilsonville, Oregon.

Page 75 from "Hart Mountain," by William O. Douglas, in *Varieties of Hope: An Anthology of Oregon Prose*, edited by Gordon B. Dodds. Copyright © 1993 by Oregon Council of Teachers of English; Oregon State University Press, Corvallis, Oregon.

Page 76 from "Tickets to Paradise," by Andy Dappen. Published in *Pacific Northwest*, April 1993.

Page 85 from *Profiles of Oregon: An Anthology of Articles from Oregon Magazine*, edited by Win McCormack. Copyright © 1986 by New Oregon Publishers, Inc., Portland, Oregon.

Page 87 from *Timber Country*, by Earl Roberge. Copyright © 1973 by The Caxton Printers, Ltd., Caldwell, Idaho.

Page 89 from *Sometimes a Great Notion*, by Ken Kesey. Copyright © 1963 by Ken Kesey; Penguin Books, New York.

Page 95 from "Cycling Crater Lake National Park," by Donna Ikenberry Aitkenhead. Published in *Bike Report*, September 1990.

Page 111 from "Bicycling Oregon's Redwoods," by Donna Ikenberry Aitkenhead. Published in *Oregon Coast*, June/July 1989.

Page 113 from "Night on the Desert," by John W. Evans, in *Oregon East*, Edited by Ronald A. Ragsdale. Copyright © 1985 by ASBEOSC, La Grande, Oregon for *Oregon East* magazine; Eastern Oregon State College, La Grande, Oregon.

Page 120 from *Stepping Westward: The Long Search for Home in the Pacific Northwest*, by Sallie Tisdale. Copyright © 1991 by Sallie Tisdale; Henry Holt & Company, New York.

Beach walkers savor the day's last light at Haystack Rock on Cannon Beach RUSSELL LAMB

66 *The easy, simple sea rolls in foamy and ruffled to a crescent of camel sand, and the mist is mere shreds of light. Everything from single rocks to single trees is outsize, overlarge, bizarre and solitary and old. A bank of clouds on the horizon seems without definition, out west as far as west can go, and the sun turns it into a dreamy cloud of gold.* **99**

Sallie Tisdale,
Stepping Westward:
The Long Search for Home in the Pacific Northwest